DANISH DINNER PARTY

TRADITIONS AND RECIPES

BY RICHARD E. KLEIN

with selected illustrations by
Ellen Joanna Møller Kristensen Klein

Published by Dumb Dickie Press

The Dumb Dickie Press logo is a trademark of Richard E. Klein.

ISBN-13: 979-8-6777-2556-2

Cover design by Ellen Meyer and Vicki Lesage

Menu

A TRADITIONAL DANISH HOLIDAY DINNER

HORS D'OEUVRES

Nuts & Gløg

APPETIZER

Smørrebrød med fisk   or   Blomkålsuppe
(Spread bread with fish)   (Cauliflower Soup)

ENTREE

Flæskesteg med Svær   &   Æbler og Svedsker
(Roast Pork with Crackling)   (Baked Apple and Stewed Prunes)

Rødkål   Brunede Kartofler
(Red Cabbage)   (Potatoes with Caramel Sauce)

Agurkesalat   Græskar
(Cucumber Salad)   (Pumpkin Rind Pickles)

DESSERT

Risalamande   or   Æblekage
(Almond Rice Pudding)   (Apple Cake)

Kaffe og Kransekage
(Coffee and Almond Ring Cake)

Table of Contents

Introduction

In 1986, I decided to host a traditional Danish dinner party, with all the pomp and circumstance I could manage.

As a child, I was exposed to Danish traditions since my mother is from Denmark. I had been in awe of the grandeur and ceremony of the formal dinner and wanted to recreate that experience as an adult. My goal was to host an authentic Danish dinner for 10 guests and share my Danish heritage and pride.

In this book, I explain Danish customs and present a full menu for a traditional dinner, complete with genuine rituals for each step of the evening. I also provide authentic Danish recipes for each item on the menu, including a few alternate recipes and variations. After reading, you'll be able to host the perfect traditional Danish dinner yourself, or simply share your newfound knowledge of Danish traditions with your friends.

"To gain a full understanding"

To gain a full understanding of a "typical" formal Danish dinner, it's helpful to learn more about the Danes themselves. The Danes, as well as the other Scandinavians, are a people with what at first appears to be a rather simple eating style, but deeper inspection reveals an array of complex foods and an equally complex social and cultural structure.

Danish people are known for *hygge*, a somewhat nebulous word that can mean well-being, finding happiness in the little things in life, contentment, being present in the moment, or a simple feeling of comfort and joy. This attitude is exemplified by the traditional dinner. Though formal and proper, the dinner party is also where we can enjoy the companionship of loved ones and the comfort of traditions, promoting the experience of hygge. That is the experience I sought for my own guests and hope you can share with yours, too.

My childhood recollections were hazy, however. I remember the formality of the events, and also the conviviality shared by the guests. Although the gatherings were very ceremonial, with each person playing his or her role, it was obvious to me that the adults derived considerable pleasure from the experience.

"My childhood recollections are hazy"

Despite having observed these gatherings in my childhood, I still wasn't sure how to start planning my own dinner party. So I began with a conversation with my Danish-born mother, Ellen Joanna Møller Kristensen Klein, asking her to recall all the mealtime and drinking rituals she could.

My mother was born in northern Denmark on the inland sea island of Mørs. She left Denmark in 1926 as a 12-year-old child, moving from the idyllic countryside in Denmark to an urban setting of filthy docks, slums of the American East Coast, and the poverty of the 1930s economic depression. Thus, she always painted Denmark as the ideal place and Danes as the ideal people. Mother bestowed valuable information about 1920s Danish customs from her own childhood and young adulthood.

As an aside, my mother was deeply attached to her grandmother's farm, common people engaged in daily activities, and farm animals. My mother's paintings commonly depicted farm life. Ocean and water scenes were also a part of her art subjects. Mother feared but also deeply respected geese. Geese are strongly territorial and are thus akin to watch dogs. In her later life in America, she painted and sketched geese. In her art circles she became known as The Goose Lady. Some sketches of geese by my mother are incorporated in this book.

"Mother's paintings commonly depicted farm life"

In addition to relying on my own memories and input from my mother, I queried my acquaintances who had lived in Denmark in various time periods. Denmark has changed vastly over time, and that change is evident in the different views taken from the 1920s, the 1950s, and the 1980s. In this book, I attempt to blend those views while at the same time maintaining authenticity.

I drew from extensive personal correspondence in the 1980s with Professor Spencer C. Sorensen. Dr. Sorensen is a Danish-American raised in Wisconsin. He was a colleague of mine for many years at the University of Illinois. He is wed to a Danish woman, Ingelese, and now resides in Lyngby, Denmark. He and Ingelese graciously reviewed the crude initial drafts of this book and made many suggestions. I am deeply appreciative of their assistance, which is enhanced by Professor Sorensen's dual status as both a Dane and an American.

Also in the 1980s, I gained helpful insights from a personal interview with Curtis O. Pedersen. Dr. Pedersen, another fellow professor and colleague of mine at the University of Illinois, was a Danish-American raised in Minnesota and generously shared his knowledge of Danish customs.

My final contributor was Ms. Lise Davis, a Dane who spent her first 20 years in Denmark before moving to the U.S. in the 1950s. I've included a letter from Ms. Davis (Appendix B), wherein she gives her own personal and informative remembrances as a young lady in Denmark.

"The Danes are a somber lot"

In reference to the Danes and their culture, Lise Davis once remarked in a telephone conversation with me that the Danes are a somber lot, but they can loosen up with a few drinks, especially at a good funeral. I wish to extend a special thanks to Ms. Davis for her kind assistance with research. She also furnished many of the recipes, graciously loaning me her own well-used cookbook with the note, "Herewith my tattered Danish Cookbook, which my daughter decorated many years ago. Please return when you have finished with it, as it is useful from time to time."

In the end, I hosted a successful and authentic party, using the menu that follows. A wonderful time was had by all. And now I am providing you with everything you need to learn about Danish customs and host your own traditional Danish dinner.

Skål!

Danish Customs and Dining Rituals

TO HOST YOUR OWN Danish dinner party, you must learn more than just the recipes—you must learn about the culture, customs, and rituals of the Danes. You must embrace the concept of hygge so that you can bring it into your own home and infuse it into your party.

This book centers on the Danes, though close parallels carry over to the other Scandinavian cultures, primarily the Swedes and the Norwegians. The Finnish people are somewhat more removed from the Danish customs discussed herein. The Finns are descended from Hungarian/Turkish bloodlines, but Finland was a part of Sweden for approximately 600 years, from the 1200s to the 1800s. Thus the Scandinavian influence on the Finns.

Several other groups of Scandinavians exist, notably the Icelandics and the Faeroe Islanders. Both of these latter groups are closely related, cuisine-wise as well as culturally, to the Danes.

Eating

ADHERING TO TABLE RITUALS and other social graces is of utmost importance to the Danes and all Scandinavians.

The Danes don't traditionally snack prior to a meal; serving hors d'oeuvres is rare. When Danes are ready to eat, they sit at the table as opposed to hovering near munchies and drinks. They also don't sit around balancing plates on their knees, with a beverage in one hand and a napkin and utensils in the other. In Denmark, one sits down to eat at a real table.

When a before-dinner drink is served, the fare is limited to a few nuts and one drink (never two). The host and hostess serve dinner promptly. The appetizer course is often on the table when the guests arrive.

Danes traditionally commence the evening dinner around 6:30 to 7:00 p.m. Guests are expected to be punctual. If you are invited for dinner at, say, seven o'clock in the evening, this means you arrive at "the stroke of seven" of the clock. Imagine a standing grandfather clock prominently displayed in the home. Guests will time their arrival as the clock chimes the seventh time.

"Guests are expected to be punctual"

Many Americans think of a Scandinavian dinner as a lavish *smørrebrød*, but that's a myth. Smørrebrød means "spread bread," or more loosely, a table of buttered bread sandwiches. This is associated with a midday lunch where one has lots of choices and distinct courses aren't necessarily obvious. The Swedish equivalent is the *smörgåsbord*, which has been more popularized in the United States.

A formal state or family dinner, on the other hand, consists of a number of specific courses along with proper ceremony, served in the evening. The smørrebrød may also refer to the appetizer course, but only if spread (buttered) open-faced sandwiches are served.

The Danes usually serve three courses with the traditional dinner: an appetizer, the main course, and then dessert. Coffee and cookies (or something sweet) are served afterward, and are not counted as a course, per se. It is expected that clean plates will be brought out for each successive course. All the silverware is placed on the table in advance in the intended order of use, so that guests use fresh silver for each course. For the formal Danish dinner party, this means sterling silverware. The hostess uses her best china dishes.

Like many Danes, my grandmother had a china cabinet filled with ample sets of china. An elegant tablecloth was always used for dinner parties, along with folded cloth napkins. Sterling napkin rings were common. Even the attire of the guests was fitting. Men commonly wore three-piece suits. The ladies wore fine dresses. Elegance ruled the day.

The quantity of food served usually exceeds what will actually be consumed. According to custom, the good host and hostess desire to provide amply and thus no guests will ever be able to eat all that is prepared.

"Enhance the festive mood"

This abundance of food may at first glance appear wasteful, however this is not the case. Leftover foods eventually make their way into other dishes, such as soups and casseroles. Danish cuisine relies heavily on the use of leftovers in many forms, but leftovers are not, of course, part of a formal dinner.

Dining rituals are as much a part of the dinner as the food itself. These rituals serve to enhance the festive mood, and their enactment forms or strengthens the relationships among the participants.

Good Danes would have name places—or at least a seating plan—prepared in advance, as opposed to leaving it to chance or burdening their guests with the decision. Much thought goes into the table plan so that everyone sits next to a person that he or she will find pleasant and entertaining, as the dinners can be quite long affairs.

"Dinners can be quite long affairs"

The Danes (and all Scandinavians for that matter) are very taciturn and formal people when in the presence of anyone other than the most intimate of friends and closest of relatives. For example, traditional Danes, even at the midpoint of the 20th century, would refrain from using first names in conversation in the presence of others. The Danes would instead address each other rather formally, such as "Miss Møller" even while speaking directly to Miss Møller. This was true even if they had known Miss Møller for decades, had cared for her during years of illness, and knew that her name was really Martha. When I visited my great-aunt in 1971 she was addressed by non-family as "Miss Møller." Because I was family, it was proper that I could address her as Aunt Martha. My mother used the Danish translation for aunt, which is moster. In recent years, these strict social rules have softened considerably.

Drinking

NO MEAL IS COMPLETE without its accompanying drinks. There is as much tradition with Danish drinking as there is with the meal and food itself.

The traditional Danish drink of *akvavit* (or aquavit), a vodka-type drink flavored with caraway, is often served with lunch or snack or a midday smørrebrød, but rarely, if ever, at an evening dinner. When akvavit is served, it should be presented chilled by icing the bottle down or even freezing cold (by putting the bottle in the freezer). Akvavit is most common with lunch and most often with fish dishes, although Danes will frequently continue to drink akvavit through the rest of the lunch.

Another traditional Danish drink to accompany a lunch is Danish beer, such as Carlsberg or Tuborg. At a luncheon smørrebrød, beer is often used as a chaser to follow the akvavit.

"Wine has become most common"

The Danes have borrowed much of their present-day cuisine from the French, including white wines, red wines, and cognac. The French influence on Danish food started several centuries ago among the upper social classes and has more recently filtered down to the general population. The French Revolution motivated French cooks to leave France and seek employment elsewhere. What is presented herein is representative of traditional Danish cuisine prior to continental or French influence, except for the inclusion of appropriate wines and cognac. Thus, wine has become most common with dinner, although in the countryside beer can still be served.

A meal has special formalities, especially to do with drinking. The strict rules apply to "snaps" or akvavit, which may be served with the smørrebrød, as well as to wine which is served with the dinner. Each course of beverage requires a fresh glass, with the correct size and shape for each. As you are expected to empty your glass, it should not be too large, nor filled too much.

You start to drink only in a prescribed manner and according to a ritual. The ritual has three distinct stages:

1. The *skål* (pronounced "skoal") and the "first look"
2. The actual drinking, or gulping, of the spirit
3. The "second look"

The host commences the initial skål after everyone has had a few bites. Danes like to drink, but not on an empty stomach. The host gives a "skål" by raising a glass as a suggestion of welcome to all those seated at the table. Then all guests look directly into the eyes of the host (the "first look") with glasses poised in hand and reply back with a "skål." All look at each other and nod beginning with the host or the person proposing the toast. The host returns a look to each person individually by a scanning eye contact around the table as the glasses are still raised. Appropriate nods of recognition of the "looks" take place during this phase. This completes the first portion of the ritual.

The second portion, the actual drinking of the spirit, then occurs. The glass is drained in one gulp once the ritual of the first look is complete.

The third and final phase of the ritual, the tradition of the "second look," follows after all have consumed their mandatory drink. They immediately make eye contact again with the host. The host makes a second scan around the table, acknowledging each guest one at a time, and then a final nod of recognition, followed by nods in reply from the guests.

Once the first skål ritual (with all of its three phases and looks) is complete, guests are permitted to initiate additional rounds of "skål." Each male guest has a duty to skål the lady on either side of him at the table, and also the lady across the table from him, at some time during the dinner.

In the process of skåling, each consumes a glass full of spirit, and thus some degree of intoxication may result. The hostess is exempt from being skåled repeatedly, otherwise she would soon be "under the table" if all guests skåled her.

"Some degree of intoxication may result"

It is this author's belief that the skål and associated looks are also required for the wine, however the full gulp may be replaced with a respectable sip. The Danes then continue to sip wine such as the French or Americans sip wine with the meal.

It's common in larger groups to skål within a smaller group, such as those at one portion of the table, but only after the initial skål with the entire group has taken place. It is a serious social error to drink at the table in a haphazard manner.

These rules apply to both akvavit and wine. The rules for beer, however, are very relaxed.

Many Americans wonder about the translation of the word "skål." If you are squeamish, I advise you not inquire into the meaning of the word. A discussion of skål can be found in Appendix A.

Singing

DANES ENJOY SINGING TOGETHER, especially at the close of a meal while they are still gathered around, and it's not uncommon for traditional Danes to end up singing a song known as "Han Skal Leve" which is roughly equivalent to the American "For He's A Jolly Good Fellow." The Danish title translates literally as "He Shall Live."

"Danes enjoy singing together"

Han Skal Leve is very common at special occasions, such as a birthday party. A speech will be made in honor of the person celebrating, then at the end of the speech, the speaker proposes a skål and three "hurrahs" for the person being honored. At the end of the hurrahs, the group starts singing Han Skal Leve. If the object of the praise is a woman, the words are "Hun skal leve" as "hun" is the feminine version. If a couple is being toasted or celebrated, such as an anniversary, then the words are "De skal leve" as "de" means "they."

Five choices for providing the music are:

1. To demonstrate the modern state of the Danes, Professor Sorensen developed an IBM PC computer program in BASIC that plays the tune to Han Skal Leve. See Appendix C for detailed instructions for creating and executing the program.
2. Obtain a recording of someone else playing.

3. Play the tune on your piano.

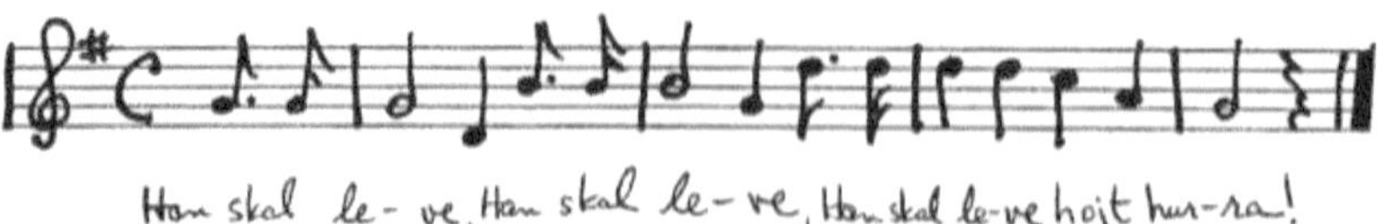

4. Go to YouTube and search for "Han Skal Leve." A number of options will appear with groups of people singing the song. Select your favorite.
5. Contact the author in advance who will sing it over the phone so that you will learn the tune yourself.

A number of other songs might also be sung at a traditional Danish dinner, but this is the only one I know.

Tobacco

OLD-TIME DANES, including the women, would complement the meal by lighting up a smoke while still seated at the table between courses, and also after the meal during coffee. The Danes have always had a traditional weakness for tobacco. The host usually supplies the cigarettes and cigars, which can be passed around to the guests. The men would have a cigar, and the women would have either cerutes (a small cigar or cheroot) or cigarettes.

Some modern Danes who choose not to smoke do not comply with this practice. In the earlier days of the prior century it was not uncommon to see traditional Danish women smoking on small cigars, although this is far less common now.

At my grandmother's house, after dinner the men smoked cigars while the ladies hand washed the dishes in the kitchen. Of course, upper crust Danes had domestic servants.

"A traditional weakness for tobacco"

Manners

DANES BY TRADITION are a rather proper people. The properness is particularly evident in their eating practices. As you've learned thus far, a traditional or family dinner has a relatively fixed format. To understand Danish cuisine, it's important to know that there is a proper way to do things, and a proper way to eat in particular.

Danes who visit America are taken aback when they find out that we eat hamburgers with our fingers as opposed to using a knife and fork, which is the "proper" way to eat a hamburger. Younger generations of Danes, however, are becoming more knowledgeable about American ways and are more adaptable.

"Guests are expected to act properly"

Danes, like other Scandinavians, take the pleasures of eating very seriously. The gathering together of friends and family for a festive meal is an occasion to be marked by dignity and ceremony. Proper presentation of the food is vital to the Danes along with adherence to a number of social graces and customs. Guests are expected to act properly, and the host and hostess also must act properly. For example, a proper guest will bring fresh cut flowers for the hostess, and the hostess, properly anticipating this, will be ready with an assortment of vases, just in case.

There are special rules for thanking the hostess for the meal, and for protocol in general. For a formal dinner, the guest seated to the left of the hostess is obliged to make a little speech of appreciation on behalf of all present, especially at special occasions such as weddings, birthdays, and anniversaries. In the initial speech, the hostess is thanked and praised for the excellent food, and the host is praised for the excellent wine. If subsequent speeches are given, there is an order of who speaks next: 1) welcome by those being honored, 2) parents, sons, and daughters, and 3) friends. Speeches are held between courses. Speeches are not given for family get-togethers or with friends unless it is a special occasion.

In terms of table graces, it is polite, when passing food, to say "vaer saa god" ("be so kind"—and in pronunciation, the "d" becomes nearly silent) to the person who receives the food, who in turn replies "tak" (thank you).

Each guest must thank the hostess for the food upon leaving the table. Specifically, at the close of the meal, as one gets up from the table, each guest says "Tak for mad" (pronounced "tock for mot") to the hostess, which translates as "Thank you for the meal." The hostess usually replies "Vel-be-komme" which means "May it become you well." According to Lise Davis (refer to her letter in Appendix B), the hostess positions herself in the adjoining room, under the chandelier, to accept the "Tak for mad" from each guest. If one has visited for tea instead of dinner, one says "Tak for tea" and if one has visited for coffee, one says "Tak for kaffe." The hostess or host replies with "Vel-be-komme" in any case. If one has enjoyed dinner and then coffee, there are two rounds of thanks by each guest in the course of the evening, one for dinner, and the second for coffee.

Danish immigrants to the United States for the past century have tended to come from the rural and working classes. As such, these people did not bring with them as high a social structure and cuisine as discussed herein. But most Danes, of whatever class or social background, make an effort to act with dignity.

"Make an effort to act with dignity"

When this dinner is put on for a gourmet group on a shared basis, various participants may assist with the cooking tasks. However, the hosts are always responsible for gløg (a beverage), coffee (must be strong to be authentic), alcoholic beverages, water, table service, "cigars" (I recommend that you locate candy cigars* to pass around as few Americans want to sit in a room with 12 cigar smokers, let alone smoke themselves) and some means of playing or reproducing the tune to the Danish song "Han Skal Leve."

The host couple is strongly advised to read the previous sections in this book, with particular emphasis on the eating traditions, the skål ceremonies, the seating of guests, and the presentation of the table. The hostess is advised to have a selection of vases ready should any of the "proper" guests bring flowers.

The host is also responsible for providing a modest supply of nuts and chips.

*Fannie May Candies usually carries chocolate cigars.

Christmas Traditions

For a traditional Christmas dinner, the host would have a Christmas tree. In Denmark of old, the ornaments would be real candles. For modern times and lacking the courage to use actual candles, small clear lights may be used to ornament the tree. Colored lights would *not* be used.

The mother of the author tells that one would only light the candles on the tree when someone was present in the room, and a bucket of water would be kept handy just in case.

"A bucket of water would be kept handy just in case"

Risalamande (rice pudding) is the traditional Christmas dessert in Denmark. A whole almond is hidden inside the pudding as it is being made. The person (usually a child as the cook arranges this outcome in advance) who is lucky enough to get the portion with the almond wins a prize. The edible prize is traditionally a marzipan candy in the shape of a pig, with a red bow tied around its belly.

A Traditional Danish Menu

TIME TO PUT ON YOUR CHEF'S HAT and start cooking! Here I share a specific menu for a traditional Danish dinner, one that would typically be served during the holiday season. I've included detailed recipes so that you're prepared to host your own Danish dinner party.

A traditional Danish dinner party has 12 persons present (usually 6 couples) and so all recipes are for 12 servings (or more). Remember, the Danes always like to prepare more than will be needed! The recipe units have been converted from European measures to American measures for the convenience of the American cook.

A Non-Course

A FEW NUTS AND CHIPS may be served with a drink (remember, only one) such as white wine or cocktails. Another suitable beverage, but only during the holidays, would be gløg, which is a heated red wine with a little rum, almonds, raisins, cinnamon, and some other spices. Gløg (glögg in Swedish) is more of a Swedish custom, but the Danes also partake of it during the holidays. Many have questioned the authenticity of gløg at a Danish gathering, but the Sorensens (who must be accepted as the author's most authoritative source) say that gløg belongs.

Using a decorative or valuable kettle for making gløg is discouraged as you will find that the flaming process can cause considerable damage to the vessel. I recommend a stainless steel kettle. The gløg will need to age for at least a week, so be sure to plan ahead.

This "non-course" isn't part of the formal meal and is therefore not served at the dinner table. There must be a decent place where the guests may sit, which can be a more relaxed setting, such as a living room.

"A decent place where the guests may sit"

Gløg (Mulled Wine)

2 bottles claret wine
2 bottles port
2 Tbsp. grated dried or candied orange peel
20 cardamom seeds
5 or 6 cinnamon sticks
25 cloves
1 lb. blanched almonds
1 lb. seedless raisins
1 lb. lump sugar
1 bottle cognac

Pour the claret and port into a large copper kettle (nickel or silver-lined) and heat slowly. Put the orange peel, cardamom seeds, cinnamon, and cloves into a cheesecloth bag, then place the bag in the kettle. Boil very slowly for 15, add the almonds and raisins, heat another 15 minutes. Remove the kettle from the heat; remove the spice bag.

Place a wire grill over the kettle and put the sugar on the grill. Gradually pour the cognac over the sugar. Hold a lighted match near the sugar and the cognac will flame it. When the sugar is melted, remove the grill. Extinguish the flame on the gløg by covering the kettle.

Once the gløg cools, store in glass containers or bottles and let it age anywhere from 1 day to 1 week.

When ready to serve, reheat the gløg in a pot on the stove, then ladle into mugs and serve with a few almonds and raisins in each.

Makes 20 to 50 servings.

Kamma's Glögg (Hot Swedish Alcoholic Drink)

This recipe is from Mrs. Kamma Ugro, of Bridgeport, Connecticut. Kamma Ugro is of Swedish extraction, and she claims that this is a very Swedish recipe.

6 cardamom seeds
6 slices of citrus rind
2 cinnamon sticks
3 cloves
12 blanched almonds
1/4 cup each raisins, currants, prunes, and dried apricots
1/2 gal. of sherry or claret wine
rock candy, about 1 lb. or the equivalent in sugar cubes
1 qt. brandy (or akvavit)
1/2 gal. of port

Place all solids in a cloth napkin or a piece of cheesecloth (or use an immersible strainer) and simmer in the 1/2 gallon of sherry or claret for 1 hour.

Remove solids from the liquid and pour the liquid into a silver (or chemically inert) bowl. (A glass, Corningware, or Pyrex bowl is also suitable.) Discard the solids except for the almonds, raisins, and currants.

Cover the bowl with a rack (such as a metal cooling rack for cakes). Put the lumps of rock candy or lump sugar on the rack, then pour the brandy or akvavit over the candy/sugar. Ignite the liquid in the bowl and allow it to flame until the candy/sugar drips through the rack. This will take about 5 to 10 minutes.

Add the fruit solids (which had been saved above) and also add the 1/2 gallon of port, which may be at room temperature if the glögg is to be stored, or the port can be heated some in advance. It is better if the glögg is made up ahead of time and allowed to age at least a day or two, and up to a week. The glögg can also be bottled. The glögg should be reheated and served hot, in the same manner that hot buttered rum is served hot. It is okay if the glögg is burned slightly.

Makes 30 small servings (4 oz. each).

Variation: Kamma Ugro sometimes cuts the candy/sugar down to just 3 oz. so that the glögg isn't so sweet.

Course 1: Appetizer

I AM PROPOSING THREE OPTIONS for the appetizer course, but only one should be served at your dinner. Given the choice, and all other things being equal, either of the fish dishes (*Smørrebrød med fisk*) are preferred and more representative of Danish tradition. When serving fish, remember the Danish saying that a fish must swim three times: once in water (the sea), once in butter, and once in spirits (to swim in the stomach with fine wine or spirits). The Danish open-faced sandwich is an exclusive Danish tradition, for which the Danes are famous worldwide in cuisine circles.

"A fish must swim three times"

Option 1: Salmon on White Bread

In the recipes that follow, I provide two variations on salmon. One is as simple as a piece of salmon on buttered white bread garnished with lettuce or lemon. Any Danish open sandwiches must be prepared just prior to serving as freshness is important. The salmon sandwiches are eaten, most properly, with a knife and a fork.

Smørrebrød med Laks (Salmon on Buttered Bread)

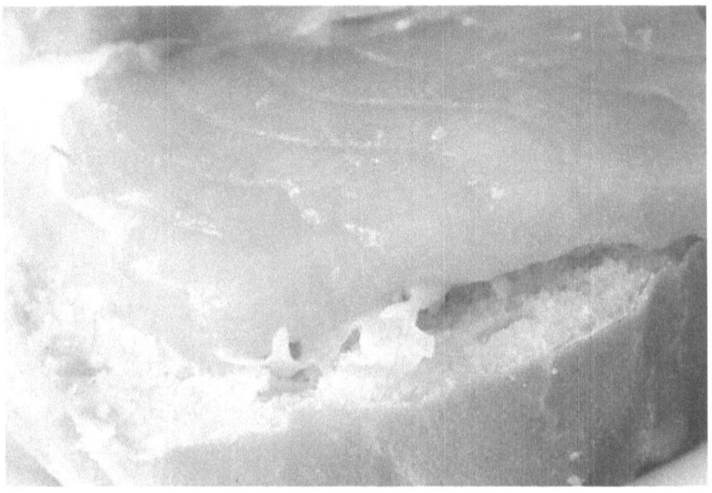

2 loaves French bread
1 stick butter, softened
1/2 head lettuce
1 lb. salmon fillets, sliced
1 lemon, cut into wedges

Cut the French bread into thin slices. Butter generously. Top with a leaf of lettuce, then top with a piece or two of salmon—enough to nearly cover the bread. Garnish with a lemon wedge.

Makes 12 to 16 servings.

Variation: The fresh salmon may be substituted with canned salmon.

Saltlaks (Salted Salmon)

3 lbs. fresh salmon or 2 lbs. salmon fillets
2 1/2 Tbsp. sugar
2 or more Tbsp. coarse salt
1/4 tsp. saltpeter
1 tsp. crushed peppercorns
6 to 7 sprays fresh dill
French dressing or skarpsås

If using fresh salmon, clean the salmon, removing head and tail, viscera, and bones. Discard everything but the fillets, which should be free of all bones and skin. Mix all ingredients except the dill and sauce, and rub the mixture into the fillets. Chop half of the dill and spread over the pieces. Lay two pieces together. Put more dill under the pieces and over them. Press between two boards with a weight on top. Keep in the refrigerator overnight.

When ready to serve, wash the fish and cut in serving-size pieces at a slant. Arrange on a serving dish, garnish with fresh dill, and serve with French dressing or skarpsås on the side. (Three recipes for skarpsås follow.)

Makes 20 or more servings.

Skarpsås med Sennep (Mustard Sharp Sauce)

6 egg yolks
1 1/2 cups olive oil
3 Tbsp. vinegar
4 tsp. French mustard
3 tsp. English mustard
3/4 cup finely chopped dill
1 1/2 tsp. salt
3/4 tsp. pepper
4 tsp. sugar

Beat the egg yolks with the oil; gradually add the vinegar, a few drops at a time, beating steadily. Beat in the mustards and dill, then the salt, pepper, and sugar. Mix well and chill. Serve with saltlaks.

Makes 12 or more servings.

Skarpsås med Fløde (Creamy Sharp Sauce)

1 1/4 cups heavy cream
2 1/2 cups mayonnaise
2 Tbsp. chopped dill

Whip the cream and combine with the mayonnaise. Just before serving add the dill. Serve with saltlaks.

Makes 12 servings.

Skarpsås med Fløde og Sennep (Creamy Mustard Sauce)

2 hard-cooked egg yolks
2 raw egg yolks
2 tsp. French mustard
1/2 tsp. Worcestershire sauce
2 cups best olive oil
3 Tbsp. wine vinegar
1 tsp. pepper
1 tsp. salt
1 tsp. sugar
1 1/4 cups heavy cream
2 Tbsp. chopped dill

Smooth and blend together the hard-cooked egg yolks and raw yolks. Mix with mustard; add Worcestershire sauce. Gradually blend in olive oil. Alternate the additions of oil with wine vinegar; season with pepper, salt, and sugar. When smooth, whip the cream, fold in, then add the dill. Serve with saltlaks. More mustard makes a sauce especially good with pickled salmon.

Makes 12 servings.

Option 2: Prawns on Buttered Bread

Prawns (small shrimp) make one of the best Danish sandwiches, which features the pale, fresh Danish fjord shrimp. The Danes call the shrimp sandwich *rejer dobbelt belagt* (shrimp doubly heaped) as they make every effort to pile on ample shrimp. And they use the term "tooth butter" in referencing the amount of butter to use; it means that the layer of butter is sufficiently thick that when you bite into a slice of bread, you leave definable tooth marks. The sandwich should always be eaten with a knife and fork.

Rejer Dobbelt Belagt (Prawns on Buttered Rye Bread)

2 lbs. fresh small shrimp
Sprig of dill
Sprinkling of paprika
1 stick butter, softened
2 loaves coarse rye bread, sliced
1 to 2 tsp. salt
1 tsp. pepper
3 Tbsp. lemon juice
parsley
1 lemon, cut into wedges

Boil the shrimp in their shells for just a minute or two in salted water, seasoned with a sprig of dill and a sprinkling of paprika. Allow shrimp to cool in their liquid. Once cool, the shrimp, no bigger than a thumbnail, must be carefully peeled. This is a tedious task that is best left to the experts, as it takes about 10 minutes to shell a single portion (enough for one person) of the baby shrimp. Alternatively, you can purchase pre-shelled shrimp.

Generously butter the rye bread (to "tooth butter" proportions). Mound the shrimp on top of the bread (remember to "double-heap" them!). Season with salt, pepper, and lemon juice. Garnish with parsley and a lemon wedge.

Makes 12 to 16 servings.

Variations: Canned prawns may be substituted for the fresh prawns. French bread may be substituted for the rye bread. A tart dressing may be added to the shrimp for additional seasoning.

Rejer med Mayonnaise (Shrimp with Mayonnaise)

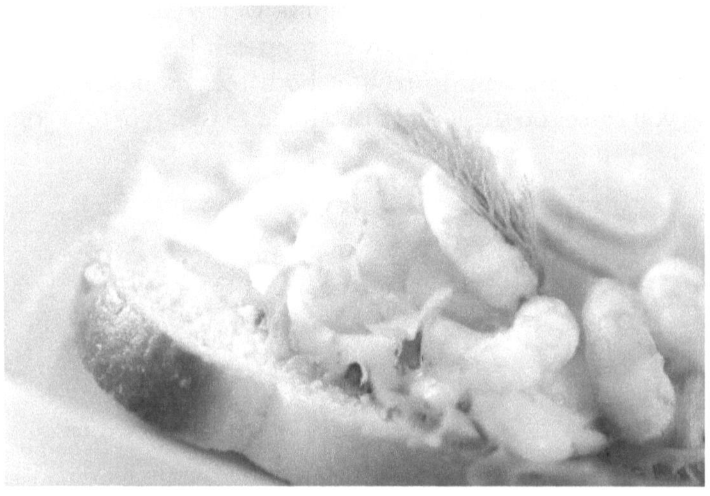

2 loaves French bread
1 stick butter, softened
2 lbs. cooked, peeled shrimp
2 cups mayonnaise
1/2 head lettuce

Cut long loaves of French bread crosswise in thin slices. Spread with butter; do not trim crust of this bread. Put finely minced and seasoned cooked shrimp around the edge of each; fill the center with very thick mayonnaise. Add a garnish of lettuce.

Makes 12 to 16 servings.

Option 3: Cauliflower Soup

If serving soup as an appetizer, it must be light, such as a clear soup with meatballs, a bouillon, or a cauliflower soup. Two recipes for cauliflower soup follow. Cauliflower soup can be somewhat tricky to make, so you might want to try out both recipes before your dinner party so you can choose your favorite—and master it before your guests arrive!

Blomkålsuppe (Cauliflower Soup)

2 large or 3 small heads cauliflower
5 quarts bouillon
1/2 cup flour
1 stick butter
7 to 9 egg yolks
1 1/2 Tbsp. salt
white pepper to taste

Divide the cauliflower into florets, boil in bouillon 10 to 15 minutes, then remove them. Stir together flour and butter, form into a ball, then place the "butter ball" into the boiling liquid.

While the butter ball is cooking, beat the egg yolks well. Optionally add cream, wine, sherry, or lemon juice to suit the flavor you're going for.

Once the butter ball has been cooked through, beat the soup well and cook for another 5 to 10 minutes. Take a little of the boiled soup and whip it into the eggs, then pour the mixture into the soup, continuing to beat strongly. The soup must not boil when the eggs are added, otherwise it will separate. Once egg yolk thickens, add up to a tablespoon of flour. Season with salt and pepper to taste.

Makes 12 servings.

Blomkålsuppe med Ost (Cheesy Cauliflower Soup)

from Brobeck and Kjellberg [1]

2 medium-sized heads cauliflower
1 1/2 sticks butter
1/2 cup flour
5 quarts stock or bouillon
salt
6 egg yolks
2 Tbsp. cold water
1/2 tsp. white pepper
1/2 cup Parmesan cheese

Wash the cauliflower carefully, cover it with salted boiling water, and cook till tender, but not too soft. Drain it; save the cooking water. Separate the cauliflower into florets and place in a tureen; keep warm at a low temperature. Stir the butter and flour smoothly together in the soup kettle. Add the stock and 1 cup of the cauliflower water; heat, stirring till well mixed and beginning to boil. Boil 3 to 5 minutes. Add a little salt if needed. Beat the egg yolks with 1 tablespoon of cold water, mix with a little of the hot stock, then add to the soup, stirring continually. When boiling, add the pepper and cheese. Pour over the cauliflower in the warmed tureen.

Makes 12 servings.

Course 2: Main Course

FOR A DANISH DINNER IN DECEMBER as the holidays approach, the main course would be goose, duck, or pork. The Danes love pork, a mainstay in all seasons. Thus, the choice of pork below is very traditional for a Danish Christmas dinner.

Danes are very particular about their pork. Danish pigs have a different diet than corn-fed American pigs. Danish pigs are fed leftover whey from the cheese-making process, along with barley and soybean meal. Consequently, Danish pork is generally much leaner than U.S. pork.

"Danes are very particular about their pork"

It's considered a treat to have the rind, or skin, still on the pork. The pork with its skin is roasted to a crispy texture, and the rind is eaten along with the pork. There is normally only a thin layer of fat between the skin and the rest of the meat.

United States meat import laws prohibit getting fresh Danish pork, so one has to be resourceful or else settle for a lean American fresh pork roast. When planning my first traditional Danish dinner in 1986, I attempted to find a specialty source for Danish-style pork in the United

States, and was able to find just one (which is all that is needed). Clausen's Deli, the shop owned by Bent Clausen in Los Olivos, California, provided excellent, genuine Danish-style fresh pork. The town of Los Olivos is near Solvang, California, the center of Danish culture in the United States. (The only rival is Racine, Wisconsin.) Over the telephone, Mr. Clausen, in his charming Danish accent, confirmed that my menu was authentic. Unfortunately, his deli is no longer in business.

Locate a pork roast suitable for the number of guests expected. One half pound of roast pork (before cooking) per person is a reasonable guide. Try to select a roast that is lean, and trim off excess fat as necessary.

As for traditional beverages, modern Danes would serve a French or Spanish red wine with the main course. Three bottles of wine should be plenty for your party of 12, especially since other beverages will be served throughout the evening.

Flæskesteg med Svær (Roast Pork with Crackling)

6 to 8 lb. fresh pork roast or loin of pork (may need 2 pieces)
salt
parsley
1/3 to 1/2 cup flour
1/3 to 1/2 cup cold water
1 cup whipped cream, unsweetened

Score the pork rind with a sharp knife lengthwise and crosswise, spacing slits 1/2 inch apart. Wash the roast in cold water, rub it thoroughly with salt, and bake it in a 350-degree oven. Put water in the bottom of the pan after roast has been in the oven at least 15 minutes, and do not baste the roast or the rind will not be crisp. Reserve the drippings.

For the gravy, heat the drippings from the roasting pan just before serving. Thicken with flour mixed with cold water. Add salt (and a little beef extract, if necessary). At the last moment, stir in the whipped cream. (No substitutes for the whipped cream—Danes always use the real thing.) Heat through and serve.

Makes 12 to 16 servings.

Æbler og Svedsker (Half Apples with Stewed Prunes)

12 apples
lemon juice
3 cups stewed prunes

Peel, halve, and core the apples. Blanch in a mixture of lemon juice and water to prevent browning. Fill the center of each half apple with stewed prunes. Bake the apples for about 30 minutes in a 350-degree oven., Be sure to not overbake them, as the apples should retain their shape as opposed to being soft.

Makes 12 servings.

Variation: Red currant jelly can be substituted for the stewed prunes.

Rødkål (Red Cabbage)

from Brobeck and Kjellberg [1]

2 medium-sized heads red cabbage
1 cup butter
1 Tbsp. sugar
1 tsp. salt
2 Tbsp. vinegar
extra vinegar, sugar, salt, and butter

Wash the cabbage and turn it upside down in salted water. Let it stand half an hour, drain, rinse, and remove any coarse outer leaves. Cut off the stalk. Slice the cabbage finely.

Melt the butter in the upper part of a double boiler, add to it the sugar, salt, and vinegar. Mix, then add the cabbage. Cover it and steam for 1 hour. Remove the cover and cook for another hour, or till the cabbage is very tender. Stir often.

Before serving, sprinkle the hot cabbage with a little sugar, salt, and vinegar mixed together and add dabs of cold butter to the dish.

Makes 12 servings.

Sød Rødkål (Sweet Red Cabbage)

sent from Denmark by Spencer C. Sorensen

1 1/2 to 2 sticks butter
3 small heads red cabbage, approximately 6 lbs.
1 1/2 cups (approximately) red beet vinegar
2 cups currant juice (or you can use currant jelly)
sugar to taste
salt to taste

Melt the butter, then lay the finely chopped cabbage in a kettle with the vinegar and butter. Cook slowly about 15 minutes under cover, turning frequently.

Add the currant juice (or jelly), then add salt and sugar to taste, and simmer until tender (about 1 hour). The red beet vinegar gives good color and taste.

Makes 12 servings.

Variations: A couple of peeled, quartered apples, and possibly caraway (Professor Sorensen notes that he is not sure about the caraway) can be boiled along with the other ingredients, as they give a good taste.

An alternative is to use a purchased red cabbage. Specifically, if you can find Aunt Nellie's brand (or equivalent) of sweet and sour red cabbage, you can save a lot of trouble as the taste is authentic.

The Sorensens suggest adding a jar of currant jelly to 2 large jars of prepared red cabbage, U.S. variety, as the jelly makes the cabbage a bit sweeter. This may be simply heated and served.

Brunede Kartofler (Sugared Browned Potatoes)

5 lbs. small potatoes
1 cup sugar
1 stick butter

The Danes are very particular about the potatoes. They must be firm, have a uniform round (spherical) shape, and be approximately equal in diameter (aim for about 1 to 1 1/2 inches in diameter).

Wash and boil the potatoes with skins on, allow them to cool and then peel, and finally rinse with water.

Melt the sugar in a pan on very low heat without stirring. When the sugar is light brown and foaming, add the butter, and when it comes to a boil again, add the potatoes. The potatoes are turned or shaken over "good heat" until they are brown on all sides and warmed through. Serve them soon, as they are not so tasty when cooled or even reheated, and they will lose their "shine" and become dull and unappealing.

Makes 12 to 16 servings.

Agurkesalat (Cucumber Salad)

2 cups water
1 cup sugar
1 cup lemon juice
1 tsp. salt
1 tsp. pepper
6 cucumbers
1/4 cup chopped parsley

Stir the water, sugar, lemon juice, salt, and pepper to make a marinade. Cut the cucumbers into very thin slices. Stir in the marinade and let the slices stand for 15 minutes. Sprinkle with chopped parsley before serving. The salad is usually served in a small bowl with a little fork used especially for the cucumber salad.

Makes 12 servings.

Variation: Vinegar can be substituted for the lemon juice.

Forår Agurkesalat (Spring Cucumber Salad)

In Denmark a "large cucumber" means about a foot and a half long, but it is only about an inch and a half in diameter, has practically no seeds or thorns, and tastes like any well-grown cucumber.

3 large cucumbers
1 1/2 cups water
1 1/2 cups vinegar
sugar to taste
black pepper to taste

Wash and dry the large cucumbers thoroughly. If using spring cucumbers, the green rind may be left on, but later in the season, when the rind is thicker and harder, it is best to peel the cucumber.

Cut the cucumber into very thin slices with a sharp knife. Mix the water and the vinegar, then sweeten to taste. Add the cucumber slices and sprinkle with pepper. Let stand for an hour or so before serving.

Makes 12 servings.

Græskar (Sweet-Sour Græskar)

A traditional side dish, at least in the author's childhood home, was græskar, a sort of sweet-sour pickled pumpkin-like rind, which is cut into small cubes about 1/2 inch on each side, or about the size of small sugar cubes or dice. The Danes grow a specific melon just for this purpose, called, of course, græskar, however pumpkin is a close substitute.

It's customary to serve græskar in a small glass side dish. Græskar serves in the same capacity as olives, pickles, and other relishes, in that it complements the meal with its distinctive sweet-sour taste.

This dish is usually preserved like pickles, so it's important that this Danish delicacy is made sufficiently ahead of time. The recipe below is for a home canning session. You will have plenty left over as you won't consume 11 quarts for one dinner party.

2 pumpkins
1 1/2 gal. vinegar
1 stick vanilla
1 ginger root
16 cups sugar
8 cups water

Cut the pumpkin into small cubes and soak for 24 hours in vinegar.

Drain thoroughly.

Cut the vanilla and ginger into small pieces. Heat the sugar and water in a large pot on medium heat until they form a syrup. Stir in vanilla and ginger. Add the pumpkin and boil until tender and clear.

Remove the pumpkin from the liquid and put into sterilized canning jars. Boil the liquid until smooth and pour over the pumpkin, then seal the jars in the usual manner as you would for pickles.

Makes about 11 quarts.

Course 3: Dessert

IN DECEMBER AND NEAR CHRISTMAS, rice pudding is common and very traditional at Danish dinners. If you are hosting your dinner party during another time of year, then apple cake would be a good option.

As for beverages, a heavier and more full-bodied dessert wine or sherry would be traditionally served with this course. In Denmark today, port, sherry, or Cherry Heering liqueur (also known as Peter Heering) would be most commonly served.

Option 1: Rice Pudding with Almonds

Rice pudding is based on rice and milk pudding to which is added chopped almonds, whipped cream, and real vanilla seeds. It's topped with a cherry sauce, lingonberry sauce, or a similar sauce that's red in color.

The name "risalamande" comes from the French "riz à l'amande," which is "rice pudding with almonds." Several different spellings are accepted in Danish in addition to risalamande, such as ris à l'amande or ris a la mande.

Again, risalamande is the traditional Christmas dessert in Denmark where children look for the hidden prize inside: a whole almond. The winner gets a marzipan pig with a red bow tied around its belly as an edible prize.

In the recipes that follow, you'll see recipes for *risengrød* (rice pudding) and *kirsebærsauce* (cherry dessert sauce), which can then be used in either of the risalamande recipes. The white rice pudding and the red cherry sauce offset each other in color and also have contrasting flavors that blend well together. I've included a recipe for *marcipan* (marzipan) as well so you can make the pig as a prize for the children.

"Children look for the hidden prize"

Risengrød (Rice Pudding)

3 quarts whole milk
2 cups uncooked rice
3 tsp. salt

Rinse a thick-bottomed pot with water before pouring in the milk. Add rice and bring to a boil. Boil covered for 45 to 50 minutes on low heat (best when it is just barely boiling), stirring frequently, all the way to the bottom. Add salt when cooking. The rice pudding must not be too thick as it stiffens somewhat when cooling. If necessary, the rice pudding can be thinned a bit with some milk.

The pudding may now be used as a main dish in this form. If so, serve with butter, cinnamon, sugar, and fruit juice or beer. If the pudding is to be used in risalamande, allow it to cool first.

Be careful with the pudding as it sticks and burns easily. Professor Sorensen says that he stirs continuously without a lid, and that his mother used a double boiler. When done, the rice must be cooked through and not hard.

Makes 12 servings.

Kirsebærsauce (Cherry Dessert Sauce)

2 cans dark cherries
2 Tbsp. cornstarch
1/2 cup water

Heat the cherries and 1 cup of the sauce from the can in a skillet; bring to a boil. Mix the cornstarch with the water, then add to the skillet. Stir the sauce until it is thickened to a gravy-like consistency. If serving right away, let cool slightly (but still warm). If preparing in advance, let cool, then refrigerate until ready to use, warming before serving.

Makes enough sauce for 12 servings of risalamande (recipe below).

Variations: Frozen or fresh raspberries can be substituted for the canned cherries. Crush them in a blender, then lightly heat them with a little sugar and lemon peel. Or you can use pre-made lingonberry sauce or a cranberry-based sauce.

Risalamande I (Christmas Rice Pudding I)

12 cups rice pudding (from the risengrød recipe above)
sweet almonds
8 to 10 leaves gelatin, according to the thickness of the porridge
1/2 stick of vanilla or 1 1/2 tsp. vanilla extract
4 Tbsp. sugar
2 tsp. sherry
2 cups whipped cream or cream

Mix the rice porridge with coarsely or finely chopped almonds. Be sure to set aside one whole almond before chopping the rest. Melt gelatin in the drained water from the rice after it has been cooked (from the risengrød recipe). Add vanilla, sugar, and sherry. Add the whole almond. Add whipped cream very gently. Pour mixture into individual glass serving dishes and let cool. They can be placed in the refrigerator until it is time to serve. Another option is to pour the mixture into a single serving bowl, refrigerate, and serve at the table from the serving dish.

Heat the cherry sauce (from the kirsebærsauce recipe) to be slightly lukewarm and serve on the table in its own dish, to be used as a topping.

Makes 12 servings.

Risalamande II (Christmas Rice Pudding II)

1 cup uncooked rice
5 cups boiling water
1 tsp. salt
4 tsp. plain gelatin
1/2 cup cold sherry
3/4 cup sugar
1 cup chopped almonds
4 cups heavy cream
4 tsp. vanilla
fruit sauce

Wash the rice and drain it. Boil water, with the salt added, then stir the rice slowly into the boiling water. Cook, without stirring, till tender. Drain, rinse with cold water, drain again.

Stir the gelatin into the sherry, then set the mixture over hot water to dissolve. Once dissolved, add it to the rice. Then stir in the sugar and almonds. Whip the cream stiff, fold in the vanilla, and mix with the rice. Pour into a wet mold. Chill for several hours.

Unmold onto a serving platter and serve with cold fruit sauce.

Makes 12 servings.

Marcipan (Marzipan)

You can use this recipe to make a marcipan pig for the Christmas pudding prize, or you can use your imagination to mold the marcipan into whatever shape you like.

1 lb. shelled almonds
1/4 lb. bitter almonds
3 3/4 cups powdered sugar
2 Tbsp. rum

Scald and peel the almonds. Let them dry, then put them twice through a grinder, using the finest knife. Add half of the sugar and grind twice again. Then work or knead in the rest of the sugar and the rum. Roll the mixture in waxed paper and put it in the refrigerator. Let stand 24 hours.

Make into small figures, roll in powdered chocolate or cocoa, or decorate with colored icing. Let stand in a cool place about 2 days before serving.

Makes about 2 3/4 pounds of marcipan.

Option 2: Apple Cake

A dessert course of *æblekage* (apple cake) is appropriate for the traditional Danish dinner. Æblekage consists of alternate layers of applesauce (preferably homemade) and toasted fine breadcrumbs. The breadcrumbs can be from any white buns, such as hot dog buns, French bread, or zwieback. The breadcrumbs are dried, crushed, mixed with sugar, and then fried with butter in a frying pan.

The æblekage is topped with little dabs of jelly (primarily as a garnish) and then served with whipped cream. Danes are a people with a strong dairy tradition, and only real whipped cream would ever be used. No substitutes, please.

Æblekage (Apple Cake)

6 lbs. apples
1 cup water (approximately)
3/4 cup sugar
1 Tbsp. vanilla sugar (see note)
1 cup dried breadcrumbs (or crushed zwieback)
1 stick butter
2 cups whipping cream
Jelly

Peel and core the apples, then boil in 1 cup of water to make a thick porridge. Add a little of the sugar and vanilla sugar to taste.

Blend the breadcrumbs and remaining sugar. Melt the butter in the pan and fry the breadcrumbs until they are golden and crisp. Stir the breadcrumbs occasionally as they cool.

The æblekage is laid together just before serving. Start with the breadcrumbs, then lay the applesauce and breadcrumbs in alternating layers in a serving dish. The top layer will also be breadcrumbs. Decorate with whipped cream and jelly (in dabs).

Makes 12 servings.

Note: Vanilla sugar can be purchased or made from scratch. To make your own, use 1 vanilla bean per 1 cup of granulated sugar. Open the bean pod(s) with a sharp knife, then scrape out the seeds and add to the sugar. Mix by hand or use a food processor until well blended.

Pour into an airtight container and add the pod shells. Allow the sugar to infuse for 2 weeks or more. It's great in coffee or tea, or sprinkled over oatmeal or toast.

Note from Professor Sorensen: The æblekage in Denmark today normally has thick layers and does not stick together as a cake, but winds up more like a pudding. What I remember from home (in Wisconsin) is æblekage made out of plain old applesauce and a breadcrumb/zwieback mixture (in layers). If done properly, you end up with an almost uniform texture that is moist all the way through.

I was told that my grandmother baked her æblekage some, but that my mother didn't. The ones I had as a child were firm enough to be turned upside down from a large mixing bowl onto a plate, and then covered with real whipped cream.

I've had æblekage served by my cousin in northern Denmark, who said it was an old recipe. It was like the modern æblekage in consistency, and not like those I remember from my mother and aunts in the United States. Whatever the source, they were sure good!

Bagt Æblekage (Baked Apple Cake)

6 lbs. cooking apples
1/2 to 1 cup sugar
1 Tbsp. vanilla
3 cups dried breadcrumbs
2 cups melted butter
whipped cream
jelly

Peel, core, and quarter apples. Simmer, covered, in a little water until soft. Force through a sieve and sweeten to taste with sugar. Add vanilla.

Butter a fireproof dish, then alternate layers of breadcrumbs and layers of applesauce in the dish, letting the bottom and top layers be breadcrumbs. Pour the melted butter down through the æblekage and bake for 30 minutes in a 375-degree oven. Turn onto a plate and decorate with whipped cream and jelly.

Additional whipped cream may be served in a separate dish. Serve the cake either hot or cold.

Makes 12 servings.

Course 4: Coffee and Almond Ring Cake

AT THIS POINT in a traditional Danish dinner (once the dinner, speeches, and dessert course are finished), the group retires to the living room or parlor for a cup of coffee, a sweet snack, and conversation. The process of getting up from the table is all quite proper, as the men rise and assist the adjacent ladies with their chairs. The first round of "Tak for mad" takes place during this movement to the adjoining room.

In the living room, one would normally be seated at a table if a table were available. If there is no table, then at minimum there should be a coffee table and/or adequate end tables. Again, Danes do not balance food on their knees while sitting on the edge of the sofa.

Kransekage (Danish almond cookies) can now finish the dinner, along with a rich and heavy coffee in small cups. Kransekage is an almond-based cookie/cake with icing. Other cookie-type delicacies can be substituted. These are more for nibbles and something sweet to go along with strong coffee. Serving a cordial or cognac is also appropriate.

Kransekage translates as crown cake. A recipe follows with instructions on how to grind and prepare the almond paste, sugar, and egg white mixture. The principal ingredient is ground almonds; the sugar, flour, and egg whites serve largely as binding agents. The paste is then formed into rings, each with a precise diameter and extending from small (about two inches) to large (about six inches). The batter is made into circular cords or strands (the cord has about the diameter of one's small finger) which are placed on molded "tins" and baked individually. Once the rings are baked and allowed to cool, the successive rings or layers are lifted off the forming pans and "cemented" one upon the other using icing both for decoration and as a binding agent. You can use a piping bag or waxed paper in a tapered roll to dispense the icing in a decorative manner.

"A set of sanity-ensuring kransekage pans"

All of my early attempts at making kransekage were fraught with difficulties until I discovered the existence of kransekage baking pans. A set of pans usually consists of six individual Teflon-coated pans, each having three concentric rings or indents. Thus with one set of pans, we can bake a total of eighteen rings of almond paste and can be assured that the rings will be the correct size. If I may be so bold, I would caution you to not even try making kransekage without a set of sanity-ensuring kransekage pans.

I acquired my set from a department store in Solvang, California for $26 in 1982. For those not going to Solvang, you can try Amazon.com. (Though if you do ever make it to Solvang, you'll be met with many Danish gift shops offering not just kransekage baking pans, but also numerous other quaint and authentic Danish goods.)

In Denmark, kransekage would usually be served at only the most festive of occasions such as a silver wedding anniversary, retirement, 75th birthday, or such. The assembled cake is actually hollow, so some opt to slide a bottle of spirits into the hollow interior portion, especially if the kransekage will be given as a gift. The icing is applied in a decorative manner to give the appearance of scalloped shingles. It's traditional to put two or more small flags on toothpick-sized sticks on top of the kransekage. At my dinner party in the United States, I used both Danish and American flags.

"I used both Danish and American flags"

The kransekage that my wife baked had a much lighter, almost whitish appearance, as opposed to the darker brown depicted in the recipe photo. The almond paste, while baking, is easily overdone to the point of burning, so be sure to watch oven times and temperatures carefully.

After baking, the kransekage should be kept in a tin that is reasonably airtight. Put a fresh crust of bread or a peeled potato in the tin a couple of days before the cake is to be served. This will give it the right chewy texture. Ring cake can be deep frozen, and then usually has the right consistency when thawed.

Kransekage is a very rich dessert food that is eaten with the fingers. You do not cut the kransekage with a knife, but rather break off a piece by hand. One starts picking at the top ring until that ring is gone, and then the successive lower rings are consumed. To maintain appearance, I suggest moving the toothpick flags to lower rings as you're eating. It would be traditional to serve coffee with the kransekage.

Danes today seldom have kransekage, but it is still a traditional food. Again, the kransekage is usually reserved for some occasion of great joy and celebration. Several years ago, my wife and I brought one to an 80th birthday party of a cousin where some visitors from Denmark were also present. One Danish lady remarked in excitement that she had not had kransekage in almost 50 years. She was delighted.

Kransekage I (Blanched Almond Ring Cake)

1 lb. almonds
1 oz. bitter almonds
3 cups sugar
4 egg whites
Frosting:
1 egg white
3/4 cup confectioner's sugar
1/2 Tbsp. vinegar

Blanch the almonds, then put them through a grinder twice. Add sugar and egg whites and mix well. When smooth, place in a pot over low heat until warm.

Shape dough into 1-inch diameter rolls, press gently with fingers to give form of a roof. Form into rings and place on a well buttered and floured baking sheet. Bake in a 325-degree oven until light brown.

For the frosting, mix egg white, confectioner's sugar, and vinegar (or lemon juice) for 10 minutes until smooth. Put into a piping bag with a fine point.

Assemble the cake starting with the largest ring and moving upwards with smaller rings. When cooled, use the piping bag to decorate with frosting, making zig-zag lines, both on the inside and outside of the rings.

Makes 1 kransekage, which should comfortably serve 12 guests.

Kransekage II (Almond Ring Cake)

1 lb. almonds
2 cups icing sugar
2 to 3 flat Tbsp. plain white flour
4 egg whites
Frosting:
1 cup icing sugar
1 egg white
2 to 3 drops vinegar

Grind almonds. Do not use a food mixer as this will result in the mixture being short and unworkable.

Preheat the oven to 400 degrees.

Mix the ground almonds, icing sugar, and flour. Work in egg whites beginning with 2 and adding 2 more in stages. The mixture must be firm but not dry.

Roll the mixture to finger-thick lengths on an icing sugar dusted board to prevent sticking, and place lengths in ring molds. Make sure they are not too thick. During baking, they will swell and if they are too thick, they can flow together. Press the ends of the lengths together thoroughly when making the rings, or they will open during baking.

Put the molds on a baking tray and bake in the middle of the oven for 10-12 minutes. Cool rapidly. As soon as rings are partly cooled, tip out of molds.

Mix icing sugar, remaining egg white, and vinegar to a thick mixture, then pipe onto rings in a thin line, zigzag pattern. Pile the rings on top of one another when the icing is dry. The rings can be fixed together with icing.

Makes 1 kransekage, which will serve at least 12 guests.

Danish Pastries

While not part of dinner, Danish pastries are world famous, and I would be remiss if I didn't mention them. Two traditional favorites are *æbleskiver* and *kringle*.

Æbleskiver

ÆBLESKIVER ARE A POPULAR MIDDAY SNACK FOOD for the Danes. Æbleskiver are made from a buttermilk and baking soda style pancake batter that is cooked in a cast iron pan with seven holes or recesses. I purchased a Griswold Danish Cake Pan back in the day, but you should be able to find other brands available today.

"A cast iron pan with seven holes"

The batter is sufficiently rich in eggs that the æbleskiver will be light. Allowing the batter to rest for up to one hour may result in a lighter, fluffier final product. Æbleskiver, which means "apple slices," are so named because the Danes traditionally added a slice of apple or a dab of applesauce during the cooking process, although the name "æbleskiver" is still used even without the apple slice cooked within.

Æbleskiver are usually served with a dusting of fine sugar (but not confectioner's sugar). It's customary to place the spherical æbleskiver in a paper bag with sugar and shake them to achieve the sugar coating. Æbleskiver are traditionally served with red jam or lemon wedges.

Æbleskiver (Danish Apple Doughnuts)

3 eggs, separated
2 tsp. sugar
1/2 tsp. salt
2 cups buttermilk
2 cups flour
1 tsp. baking soda
1 tsp. baking powder
butter
applesauce

Beat the egg yolks. Add sugar, salt, and milk. Sift together flour, baking soda, and baking powder, then add to egg yolk mixture. Fold in stiffly beaten egg whites.

Spread a small amount of butter in each cup of æbleskiver pan and fill 2/3 full of dough. Place a teaspoon of applesauce on top of dough, then cover the applesauce with a few drops of dough. Cook until bubbly, turn carefully with a fork, and finish baking on the other side. Serve with butter and maple syrup or jam.

Makes 4 servings.

Note: Be careful not to spill applesauce in the cups, as this will cause the æbleskiver to stick.

Susanne's Æbleskiver (Danish Doughnuts)

This recipe comes from a book by "Susanne" called Danish Cookery, printed in Denmark in 1950 by Host & Sons [3].

2 cups flour
1/2 tsp. salt
1 tsp. sugar
2 cups buttermilk
2 eggs, separated
1 tsp. baking soda
Butter

Mix flour, salt, and sugar. Beat together buttermilk and egg yolks. Add the flour mixture. Add baking soda and fold in stiffly beaten egg whites.

Heat the æbleskiver pan and melt butter in each hole. Pour batter into holes, but do not quite fill them. Place over low heat and turn quickly when half done. Serve very hot with jelly or applesauce on the side.

The æbleskiver look most appetizing when piled high on a serving plate and dusted lightly with confectioner's sugar.

Makes 4 to 6 servings.

Frøken Jensen's Luxury Æbleskiver
(Danish Doughnuts)

Frøken Jensen was a Danish housekeeper and cookbook writer, the Danish equivalent to America's Betty Crocker. She is remembered in particular as the author of the early Danish cookbook Frøken Jensen's Kogebog [2] (Miss Jensen's Cookbook), which has been popular for its traditional recipes since its publication in 1901.

10 eggs
1 1/4 cups cream
1 tsp. sugar
1 tsp. cardamom
1 stick butter, melted
1 1/4 cups flour
butter for frying

Whisk together egg yolks, cream, sugar, cardamom, melted butter, and flour. Fold stiffly beaten egg whites into this mixture. Bake at once in your æbleskiver pan and keep warm in the oven.

Serve with jelly or applesauce on the side.

Makes 4 servings.

Danish Kringle

A KRINGLE IS A FLAKY, OVAL-SHAPED PASTRY with fruit or nut filling. One kringle goes a long way, as one friend reported that she can serve 16 ladies for tea with just one kringle.

Genuine Danish kringle are very difficult for a novice to make, and even most gourmet cooks do not know how to prepare kringle like the authentic Danes. One has to be a masochist if one chooses to bake a kringle from scratch. Even the very Danish Midwestern relatives of this author seldom make their own kringle. Instead, they purchase one from a quality Danish bakery and store it in their freezer until they're ready to serve it. Kringle ships well, and keeps well in the freezer or the refrigerator. When guests arrive, out comes perfect kringle.

Therefore, I will not even attempt to include a recipe for this complex pastry. Instead, I suggest you order kringle from a good Danish bakery. I've listed several recommendations here, with contact information at the end of the section.

Racine, Wisconsin advertises itself as "Little Denmark" and the kringle capital of the United States. A number of bakery shops there will ship kringle via UPS, such as Larsen's Bakery in Racine. For my 1986 dinner party, I had to first contact them to obtain the appropriate mailing labels, which I then filled out and returned with my order. Delivery to central Illinois was one to two days. Now you can order directly from their website.

Another great bakery in the Racine area is Lehmann's, which sold and shipped three kringles for $14.95 back in the day. Prices have gone up a bit since then, but are well worth it for their authentic, delicious flavor. Benson Bakery in Omaha, Nebraska, now closed, was another excellent Danish pastry shop.

In the St. Louis area, I recommend Pastries of Denmark. In addition to various types of kringle, they also offer other Danish pastries and sandwiches.

On the west coast, there is little question that you'll find suitable bakeries in Solvang, California that will ship kringle. For updated information on Danish bakeries in Solvang, you can contact the Solvang Chamber of Commerce.

Pastries of Denmark
12613 Olive Blvd. West Park Center
Creve Coeur, MO 63141
pastriesofdenmark.com

Larsen's Bakery, Inc.
3311 Washington Ave.
Racine, WI 53405
larsenskringle.com

Lehmann's Bakery
9117 Durand Avenue
Sturtevant, WI 53177
lehmannsbakery.com

Bendtsen's Bakery
3200 Washington Ave.
Racine, WI 53405
bendtsensbakery.com

Solvang Chamber of Commerce
solvangcc.com

Appendix A: Origins of the Word "Skål"

WHAT FOLLOWS is for the strong of heart. According to Lise Davis, the word "skål" in Danish originates from the same language base as the word "skull"—as in human skull. You see, the Vikings were a bloodthirsty lot, and they consumed their victory celebration beverages from the human skulls of their unfortunate victims. They believed that drinking from a human skull would pass on to them strength from their deceased adversaries. Thus it might be fair to speculate that the word "skål" was, in its original context, used in the same sense as "Here's to good health, strength, and fortune." Perhaps it even suggested "May his strength now become a part of our strength."

"They consumed their victory celebration beverages"

The good Viking could only get to Valhalla, the Viking heaven, if he died in this mortal world in combat. The word "Valhalla" means "hall of the slain" in Norse mythology, and that meant slain in combat. I speculate that it could be construed as an honor to the defeated adversary to use his skull for drinking and toasting. The defeated one, who died in combat, was the lucky one to be envied as he, indeed, was assured of being in Valhalla, the utopia for Norsemen. The one drinking was in the precarious state, as his destiny was unknown. Perhaps the toast "skål" was in a way a prayer or request to be strong enough to also make it to Valhalla.

Appendix B: Letter from a True Danish Lady

October 1986

Dear Dick,

Not many people in the shop today, so I am trying to get a few lines off to you, whilst I am enjoying a lull.

You have, I know from our talk on the telephone a few weeks ago, received my small, rather tattered Danish cookbook, and I have since dug up a few more recipes for you through my pretty Danish neighbour Ulla.

Your 6 annual "binges" sound absolutely marvelous, and I bet you have a good time, even if some of the dishes don't turn out to be 100% authentic.

I have read your draft, and naughtily added lots of my own comments, which you may have to take with a pinch of salt, as I have lived abroad [outside of Denmark] for 25 years and come from an anything but normal family, although both sides gave extremely "comme il faut" dinner parties—Mother's family having more money than Father's—but both sides absolute perfectionists as to what "One Did" right down to who took whom in to dinner and having place cards, and being seated according to peerage, military rank, order of precedence, etc., so I will tell you how I remember dinners at home, and you can do what you want with that information and move into the 21st century.

You would be asked for 7 o'clock, which meant exactly what it says; if you were early, you would wait outside the gate, door, or whatever, and on the stroke of seven, the bell would be rung and a maid or host would greet you at the door, take your coat and hat and show ladies to a mirror to tidy their hair; flowers would be handed over to the staff or presented directly to the hostess, who already would be prepared with an assortment of vases just in case!!

Nowadays people may bring a good bottle of wine, box of chocolates, or even something homemade, like pâté or some other form of delicacy, then the other guests miraculously would appear, the host grabbing coats, the hostess introducing people to each other and offering a drink, and one only, as your meal would no doubt be ready to serve at 7:15 pm.

"The other guests miraculously would appear"

Old-fashioned people would serve a home-made soup, such as clear soup with meatballs and flour balls and daintily diced carrots, potatoes or whatever (always rather boring, I seem to remember) or perhaps cauliflower soup or home-made tomato, served with a dollop of cream. Richer people no doubt served smoked salmon on a piece of white bread with a bit of lettuce and twist of lemon and/or dill, and this would already await you when you were sitting down to the meal. Herewith a glass of decent German wine and then on to the main course, which after fish would be meat or game, then a good French red wine suitable for the meat; heavy Burgundy with pungent food or a Bordeaux with game or a roast; the Danes always knew their wines, and have been known to import more good red wine than any other nation in Europe (after the English, though). Nowadays you may have a decent Spanish, as good French wine has gone up in price something wicked.

A little cheese or cheese straws, straight from the oven to use up the last drops of precious red wine, and then dessert, according to season, but the dear, old applecake or lemon mousse always seemed to be favourite, apart from when we had men only to shooting parties and it was crème caramel with a light egg sauce.

The man seated to the left of the hostess would always get to his feet and raise his glass to the hostess and praise her excellent food and then turn to the host and praise him for his wine, everybody would get up, the men pulling out the chair for the women next to them and somehow the hostess would always be in the adjoining drawing room under the chandelier receiving the "tak for mad" from her guests before coffee was served in small groups around the room or even house; cigars for the men, cerutes and cigarettes for the women, a tray of liquors for everybody and coffee only served in tiny cups, hot and strong.

"The man ... would ... praise her excellent food"

Later on a tray would appear with whisky and beer and soda for the thirsty and if you played cards or danced, there would even be "natmad" [a midnight snack, usually an open-faced sandwich with butter, sliced beef, and red onion rings] often served in the kitchen, straight out of the refrigerator, unless there was staff, when small open sandwiches or "goodbye soup" was served up (bouillon). Sorry, this is very disjointed, as I keep being called away by customers or by the 'phone.

I have been very privileged to belong to a zany, fun family, so my memory of dinner parties is of sheer pleasure, dressing up and flirting madly with the men across the table or next to one, and having wonderful conversations about politics, food, travelling, and witty speeches by the various men at the table, the food was good, and served according to season, venue, purse, and occasion, but you always longed for the party, hoped to be seated next to someone nice, you dressed for the occasion and made the most of the party.

"Wonderful conversations about politics, food, and travelling"

When I go to Denmark now, sadly the older generation has died and the cousins I have are all in their 60s or 70s, so although we are still a little formal at the beginning of the meal, the wine always relaxes everybody. But, only 1-3 courses are now served up, as most people have no staff, or are poor, or can't cook if they used to have staff, or hate clearing up the next day, and as they know I love fish, we always have this or some peasant dish that I have requested!! And, being a peasant at heart, I have Ceres beer or Carlsberg or Wibroe, perhaps Albani, depending on which part of Denmark I visit at that time. As people are so figure-conscious, fruit salad is often served or a cake from the baker's emporium served with coffee before watching some 5-year-old American film on the TV. Life ain't what it used to be in the so-called good old days.

Good luck with the paperwork and of course your Christmas dinner party, ring me any time if you need more help. I will try and get my older sister in Denmark to send you the music for the drinking songs.

Best wishes from,
Lise

Appendix C: How to Run a BASIC Program

JUST FOR FUN, I decided to include Professor Sorensen's computer program that plays the tune to Han Skal Leve. Writing your own BASIC program is a bit dated when you can just search on YouTube for a video, and it might be a bit modern for a traditional Danish dinner party, but I felt it important to honor Dr. Sorensen's coding contribution as well as his recipe and customs contributions.

It's easy and fun to write programs in BASIC on your personal computer. PC-BASIC is free, cross-platform, open source software. Although it's been around in one form or another since the 1970s, it's simple and reliable. For documentation, please see the official website: pc-basic.org.

"Steps you can follow"

Here are the steps you can follow to run Professor Sorensen's program to play the song "Han Skal Leve."

1. Install PC-BASIC. You can download the software from any reputable website that offers the code for free. To find one, google PC-BASIC and follow the steps on the selected website. There are many to choose from, but I recommend this one: https://robhagemans.github.io/pcbasic/doc/1.2/. You only need to perform this step once.
2. Once the software is successfully loaded, start the interface by clicking PC-BASIC in your Start menu.
3. PC-BASIC will start in direct mode, a 1980s-style interface operated by executing BASIC commands directly. There is no menu or buttons to click as we're used to in modern software. But don't worry, even though the interface is rather primitive, it's easy to use.
4. Enter the following commands on the command line:

```
NEW
20 REM TEXT IS "HAN SKAL LEVE, HAN SKAL LEVE,
25 REM "HAN SKAL LEVE HOJT HURRA"
30 REM WHICH SOUNDS LIKE:
40 REM "HAN (AS IN HAND) SKA LEE-VAH, ETC
50 REM " HAN SKA LEV-VAH HOYT WHO-WRAH"
100 L1$=" L8 O3 G. L16 G L2 G L4 D L8 B. L16 B L2 B L4 G"
110 L2$="O4 L8 D. L16 D L4 D D C O3 A L2 G"
120 PLAY L1$+L2$
160 REM THAT'S ALL THERE IS, THERE AIN'T NO MORE!
SAVE "DANISHSONG",A
RUN
```

These commands will create a new program called DANISHSONG and will run it once. If you don't hear the tune, check to be sure your speakers aren't muted. If you still have a problem, try again, with special care to enter each line exactly as shown. Warning: You can't copy and paste—you must type in the commands manually.

To exit PC-BASIC, enter SYSTEM on the command line.

Now that the program is saved, the next time you want to play it, just open the BASIC command line (from your Start menu) and enter:

```
LOAD DANISHSONG.BAS
RUN
```

Note: If something unpredictable occurs, you can use one of the key combinations Ctrl+Break, Ctrl+Scroll Lock, Ctrl+C, or F12+B to interrupt a running program and return to direct mode.

"Something unpredictable occurs"

A Note from the Author

Dear Reader,

Thank you for taking the time to read *Danish Dinner Party*. The party I threw back in 1986 was a real hit, and I've been meaning to share my recipes and tips ever since. Now, as an 80-something-year-old retired professor, I finally had the time to do so. Wishing you all the best as you plan and prepare for your own Danish Dinner Party. Skål!

I hope you enjoyed reading *Danish Dinner Party*. If so, I'd appreciate it if you left a review on Amazon. Reviews help other readers decide to try out a new book. Just a sentence or two saying what you liked about the book will do!

Thanks again for reading and for helping get my books into the hands of other readers.

Blessings,
Richard E. Klein

P.S. Please enjoy a brief excerpt of *Second Dissertation Upon Roast Pig*, the ultimate how-to guide for hosting a pig roast.

SECOND DISSERTATION UPON ROAST PIG

PRACTICALITIES AND PHILOSOPHIES FOR THE 21ST CENTURY

RICHARD E. KLEIN, PhD

My First Pig

ONE DAY when I was a student at the University of Iowa, a friend and I thought it would be fun to host a picnic and barbecue a whole hog for a group of friends. I decided not to be intimidated by the notion of roasting a pig. I confidently began to plan and research pig roasting. In preparation, I asked many questions from the most qualified friends, received advice, and found the courage to roast my first pig.

To no one's surprise, I made many mistakes. Even with the best advice I could find, I was still guided by the false Hollywood Robinson Crusoe myth that I needed an open pit, a glowing bed of coals, and a pig skewered on a spit, slowly turned by hand all day. I learned a considerable amount that day about the stark difference between myth and reality. Since then, my knowledge, equipment availability, and skills have improved. Over my active years of roasting pig and lamb, I've roasted about 250 pigs plus 150 lambs.

Let's start with some basics. To have a roast pig cookout, it is essential that you arrange for:

1. A pig to roast
2. The equipment and know-how to roast the pig
3. Enough friends to help eat the pig and to be willing to come rain or shine

"I learned a considerable amount that day about the distinction between myth and reality"

This document endeavors to provide an overview of the process, the essential equipment, and the information required. In what follows, many aspects of pig roasting are discussed. The reader may wish to jump from place to place or from subject to subject rather than reading in the given order.

Myths and Falsehoods

A COMMON MYTH is that you must turn the pig as it roasts. However, the pig is sitting on a shelf in an oven with uniform convective heat surrounding it. The only plausible reason any meat is turned on a spit is for equalizing the heat from an uneven heat source, or to prevent scorching. In fact, any attempt to turn the pig in a roasting oven will usually cause it to fall apart, especially if the pig is near done.

The Hawaiians, famous for their luaus, bury the pig in a preheated pit lined with hot rocks, insert hot rocks wrapped in papaya leaves into the chest cavity, cover the pig, and let the pig roast with uniform heat. Hawaiians don't turn their pigs on a spit and they don't dig them up just to turn them over. What Hawaiians do is fine, but I don't have a pit filled with hot rocks, nor a supply of papaya leaves, nor the desire to have an excavation in my lawn. In any event, turning is clearly not necessary.

Another myth is that stuffing is required. If you want a stuffing, buy some Stove Top or make a homemade dressing. I recommend an apple, bread, and spice dressing, using the

Winesap variety of apple. But be sure to cook it separately. Any stuffing inserted into the pig will require you to sew up the cavity (with wire as string will be prone to burning). This reduces the effective surface area of the pig for convective heating purposes, causing it to cook more slowly because the warmed oven air can't circulate into the chest cavity. Additionally, stuffing acts as insulation, slowing the heating of the interior portions and thus increasing the possibility that the insides of the pig will spoil. Lastly, the stuffing will absorb and retain the greases given off by the pig during cooking rather than letting them drain out.

My first pig had a bread-based stuffing, but the greases so saturated it that the stuffing was not fit for human consumption. I also failed to achieve adequate internal temperatures while cooking that pig, which I attribute to the stuffing and stitched-up body cavity.

"Some old army buddies"

Some old army buddies (not cooks, like I had been) once cooked a 300-pound sow on an open spit. It took about 24 hours of cooking. In addition to the folly of attempting to cook a very large animal over an open bed of coals, they made the mistake of placing 12 fresh hams inside the body cavity and then wiring the cavity closed. They rationalized that the hams inside the body cavity would also cook (sort of, for free), but the hams as well as the insides of the pig spoiled because the temperature rise in the interior was too slow.

The Vietnamese method of roasting a pig incorporates a stuffing made up of herbs, fruits, and spices. The pig is stuffed and then coated with a special clay, which serves to seal the pig so that the flavor from the stuffing permeates the meat. The clay cracks during the roasting process, thus permitting the fat drippings to come out. The Vietnamese then discard the stuffing.

For an informative and entertaining look at how to host a pig roast, pick up *Second Dissertation Upon Roast Pig* today!

More Titles from Richard E. Klein

Second Dissertation Upon Roast Pig: Practicalities and Philosophies for the 21st Century

Shivering: Heating Up the Global Warming Debate

The Bike Whisperer: Changing the World One Bike Rider at a Time

Dumb Dickie: A Memoir of Learning, Growth, Hope, and Blunders

Kisses When I Get Home: Letters of a Long-Distance Courtship During World War II

Circling the Drain: Humorous Musings on Becoming a Mechanical Engineer

The Deadly Gamble: A Post-Mortem of the World Trade Center Collapse

Bikes Are Big on Planet Klynia (A Children's Book)

We're All Set: Selected Klein Family Memories

About the Author

Richard E. Klein, by his own admission, is an incurable romantic and altruist. His writings and musings are filled with hope and bright horizons despite having lived through World War II and the Korean War as a child, both of which deeply impacted his worldview. Through his books, he aims to point the way towards a better internal mindset and a better world.

Richard earned his Ph.D. in engineering from Purdue University in 1969 and taught systems theory for three decades at the University of Illinois in Urbana-Champaign before retiring in 1998. He holds a particular interest in bicycle stability and control, and has devoted much of his time and energy to the development of an international program for teaching children with disabilities to master bike riding. Visit RainbowTrainers.com and iCanBike.org for more specifics.

Richard and his wife of more than 55 years, Marjorie Maxwell Klein, reside in the St. Louis area. They have two children, six grandchildren, and one great-grandchild. Richard writes for them and for generations to come.

Art Credits

The author gratefully acknowledges the artwork of his mother, Ellen Joanna Møller Kristensen Klein, for the delicate pen and ink sketches of "a goose in the kitchen."

Other illustrations are reproduced from and/or inspired by the weekly paper *Apples of Gold* published by American Tract Society, New York, 1887.

One illustration with a player grand piano is from the advertising circulars of the Ampico Player Piano Company, *circa* 1920.

The above cited illustrations being a century or more in age are now in the public domain.

References

1. Brobeck, Florence and Kjellberg, Monika Brilioth, Smörgåsbord and Scandinavian Cookery, Grosset and Dunlap, New York, 1948. [This book, in English, has an excellent overview section on "Let's Look at the Menu".]
2. Frøken Jensen's Kogebog, (Miss Jensen's Cookbook) revised by Else Algreen, Else Overgaard Andersen, and Ellen M. Kelstrup Jensen, Gyldendalske Boghandel, Nordisk Forlag A.S., Copenhagen, 1966. (In Danish) [First edition is from 1701, and the edition cited is the 45th. In all, 400,000 copies have been printed.]
3. "Susanne," Danish Cookery, Andr. Fred. Host & Son, Copenhagen, 1950. (In English)

Recipe Notes

Recipe Notes

Recipe Notes

Recipe Notes

113

Recipe Notes